Giovanna Magi

ASWAN
PHILAE · ABU SIMBEL

150 Colour illustrations

BONECHI

"Egypt is the country bathed by the Nile which covers it; the Egyptians are those who, living below the city of Elephantine, drink the water of this river".

(Herodotus)

The Nile, with the villa of the Aga Khan in the foreground.

ASWAN

History

Aswan (Assuan), the ancient Syene, lies on the right bank of the Nile, 886 kilometers from Cairo.
This is where the Valley of the Nile with its typically gentle landscape ends. This is where Egypt ends and Nubia begins. Gone are the farmlands which accompany the bends of the river, replaced by endless kilometers of desert sands and the majestic still waters of Nasser Lake. The Nile too is transformed and the smooth tranquil waters give way to the sudden troubled waters leaping and eddying around the rocks of the First Cataract.
Trade and barter went on here as early as the third millennium. Nubia, whose ancient name nub (nbw) means « gold », has always been a land of conquest and exploitation. The doorway to black Africa, the only communications route between the sea and the heart of the black continent, Nubia provided the pharaohs with their best soldiers, highly prized woods, precious ivory, perfumed spices, the finest ostrich feathers — as well as gold. Syenite — that pink granite so widely used in Egyptian religious architecture in the building of temples, the sculpting

The northern tip of Elephantine Island, with Aswan stretching out behind.

Feluccas and motor-boats moored on the right bank of Aswan: in the background, left, the massive tower of the Aswan Oberoi Hotel.

The elegant Corniche seen from the river.

of colossi and obelisks — came from its many rich quarries. It was so abundant that the quarries were still in use in Roman times. Syene was also of basic importance in controlling both the river traffic and that of the desert caravans. The pharaohs maintained an armed garrison there and made Syene the capital of the first nome of Upper Egypt. The Tropic of Cancer, which now lies somewhat further south, originally passed here. Proof is the presence of a well whose straight sides are illuminated by the rays of the sun without shadows only at the summer solstice. This was how the Greek scientist Eratosthenes calculated (with a minimum of error) the length of the terrestrial meridian and concluded that the earth was round.

In early medieval times the city was subject first to the incursions of the Blemi, from Ethiopia, then fell victim to a violent outbreak of the plague. It was gradually abandoned and revived only after the Turkish conquest of Egypt. Its modern name derives from the old Egyptian « swenet » meaning « trade », transformed into the Coptic « suan » and then into Aswan.

Nowadays, in addition to its purely historical and archaeological interest, the mildness of its climate has made Aswan an ideal winter resort. Elegant hotels equipped with every imaginable comfort have risen along its banks; cruising yachts by the dozens sail up the Nile and anchor here for days at a time so that the ever growing number of tourists can visit the exceptional surroundings of the city. It is, lastly, the most important departure point for the excursion to Abu Simbel, jewel of the desert.

When evening falls, Aswan is suddenly bathed completely in violet, while the feluccas glide silently over the water, dotting the river with their enormous white sails. No other place in Egypt has the luminosity and silence that reign in Aswan.

Brightly colored cottons, repoussé copper dishes, narghilè, spices and karkadé are some of the most characteristic objects to be found in this market.

BAZAAR — The Bazaar of Aswan in atmosphere and charm is second only to that of Cairo.
Parallel to the Corniche — the avenue which runs along the Nile, shaded by tall hibiscus trees laden with red flowers — it winds through the narrow streets of the old city. One can truly breathe the air of Africa in this souk: the tall wicker baskets set on the ground are full of exotic spices and brightly colored enticing powders, from karkade to henne, from saffron pistils to curry, from red pepper to the dark-leafed mint tea. Objects in braided straw, in ebony, in ivory abound. Everywhere a teeming of dark-skinned peoples (the Nubians are thinner and darker than the rest of the Egyptian population) and a fluttering of long white garments.

Feluccas on the Nile: a bare breath of wind is all that is needed to make them glide over the water.

The southern tip of Elephantine with the construction that houses the Club Méditerranée at the center.

ELEPHANTINE ISLAND

While the rich granite quarries were in ancient Syene, most of the trade took place on the Elephantine Island. It was here that the governor of the province had his residence, and it was also the center of the cult of the ram-headed god Khnum. Originally the island was named Yebu, which means « elephant » in Egyptian. The Greeks translated it into Elephantine, probably because this was where ivory from Africa was traded. The island is 1500 meters long and 500 meters wide. It now incor-porates two typical Nubian villages and the large Hotel Assuan Oberoi as well as the Museum of Aswan and the archaeological zone of Yebu.

To land on the island one passes below enormous rocks covered with graffiti and inscriptions dating above all to the 18th (Thutmosis III and Amenhotep III) and the 26th dynasties (Psamtik II), docking at the tiny pier constructed of material that came from buildings dating to the New Kingdom.

10

The archaeological complex of ancient Yebu, on Elephantine Island.

Rock elephants, with hieroglyphic inscriptions left by travelers of old.

Eroded by the waters of the river, these rocks resemble a group of elephants.

Elephantine Island as painted by David Roberts.

The exterior of the Museum of Aswan seen from the river.

Interesting sarcophaguses in granite are housed under the veranda of the Museum.

The painted sarcophagus of the wife of a priest and a detail of the mummy of the Sacred Ram.

MUSEUM OF ASWAN — Since 1912 this small museum has been installed in the villa that belonged to William Wellicocks, the English engineer who designed the Old Dam of Aswan. In fact it has all the appearance of a charming inviting colonial house, with a veranda opening out onto the garden, flowers and plants growing all around.

The archaeological finds in the museum all come from excavations undertaken in Aswan and other sites in Lower Nubia. Of particular interest is the *mummy of the sacred ram* in a gilded sarcophagus. It dates to 330-305 B.C. and was found in a tomb right behind the museum building. Khnum was consid-

ered the creator of mankind and since he was said to have modelled the first man from the clay of a vase, he was worshipped as the patron of the potters. At Aswan he was associated in a triad with Anukis, goddess of the island of Siheyl and with Satis, goddess of the Elephantine Island. The ancients also believed that Khnum lived in a cave nearby and that this was where he hid the flood which periodically overran the island. Also to be noted is the *cosmetic palette in slate* kept in a showcase in the first room, odd in that it is in the shape of a rhinocerous which was an animal unknown in Egypt at the time.

Remains of the Great Temple of Khnum.

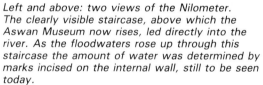

Left and above: two views of the Nilometer. The clearly visible staircase, above which the Aswan Museum now rises, led directly into the river. As the floodwaters rose up through this staircase the amount of water was determined by marks incised on the internal wall, still to be seen today.

NILOMETER — «... there are marks which measure the height of the water for irrigation. They are used by the farmers to measure the flow of the water, by the bureaucrats to establish the amount of taxes. In fact the higher the water the higher the taxes». This is what Strabo once wrote about the Nilometer, a staircase of 90 steps which went down into the waters of the Nile and made it possible to know in advance the date of the flood and the amount of water thanks to a graduated scale engraved on its walls. The inscriptions are in Greek (a scale with Arab measures was added later) and record some of the famous floods, from Augustus up to Septimius Severus.

ANCIENT YEBU — Further on, beyond the Nilometer, is what remains of the ancient city of Yebu. The main building was the **temple dedicated to Khnum**, begun in the 30th dynasty under Nectanebo II and continued under the Ptolemies and the Romans. It consisted of a court behind which was the hypostyle hall and the sanctuary. We can still see a large portal in granite with cartouches of Alexander Aegos and a naos, also of grey granite, with the pharaoh Nectanebo II worshipping Khnum.

In the vicinity, the small **temple of Heqa-ib** also came to light. Heqa-ib was a nomarch at the end of the Old Kingdom to whom his successors dedicated this small temple that consists of a court surrounded by naos-chapels, each of which contained a statue of Heqa-ib. Even further towards the southernmost tip of the island lies another **chapel of the Ptolemaic period** rebuilt by using material found in Kalabsha when the temple there was dismantled.

The Nubian village, with its characteristic colored doors. The inhabitants are extremely courteous and friendly and love talking with the tourists. At the right, a typical container for water, in which it stays cool for hours.

NUBIAN VILLAGES — Immersed in the green of the palm groves on the Elephantine Island, three Nubian villages transport us — without warning — into a different world. Here the inhabitants, extremely courteous, are always ready to offer the visitor a cup of perfumed mint tea. The houses are brightly colored in green, blue and yellow. Often the black cube of Mecca, the sacred Kaaba, is painted on the exterior, a sign that the owner of the house had gone in pilgrimage to the holy city of Mecca. Sometimes the means of transportation are also painted — a plane, a ship, a car. . .

The Ptolemaic chapel rebuilt with material from Kalabsha and a detail of the decoration of the interior.

Two enchanting views of the Nile: above, the mausoleum of the Aga Khan, and, below, the Club Méditerranée.

In the following pages:

The famous Old Cataract hotel, characteristically colonial in style: the interior with its large fans with wooden blades, the costumed waiters with their red fezzes, the plush carpets and the antique furniture takes us back to another century. The exterior of the hotel appeared in the film « Murder on the Nile », based on Agatha Christie's famous mystery novel.

The Aga Khan's mausoleum silhouetted against the sky at sunset.

Sunset on the Nile.

KITCHENER ISLAND

North of Elephantine is the Island of Trees, better known as Kitchener Island. Lord Horatio Kitchener was an English general who had fought valiantly in the Sudan in 1898, defeating the army of the Mahadi. Consul General in Egypt, he fell in love with this island in the middle of the Nile, where he could give free play to his passion for exotic flowers and plants. This spendid botanical garden contains the rarest examples from Africa and Asia: a symphony of colors and fragrances accompany us in our leisurely wanderings along shady avenues. Bougainvilleas and poinsettias, hibuscus and clematis, mangoes and sycamores. fragrances that are pungent or subtle, shades of color ranging from brilliant reds to delicate pinks.

Birds also love this enchanted garden and live here undisturbed among the bushes and the underbrush. In the southern part of the island, a tiny bay populated by white ducks has been created under a lovely terrace where one can sip karkade in blessed peace.

Three aspects of the luxurious vegetation on Kitchener Island.

The delicate pink sandstone of the mausoleum contrasts with the green palms and gardens below.

Feluccas on the Nile.

In the following pages, the entrance to the Aga Khan's mausoleum and the blue stretch of water dotted by the white sails of the feluccas.

MAUSOLEUM OF THE AGA KHAN

In 1957 the Aga Khan III Mohammed Shah, spiritual head of the Ismailian Muslims, died. This community, whose center is in India, has about four million followers, scattered throughout the world. Extremely rich (the day of his jubilee his weight was equalled in diamonds), he used to spend part of the winter in this villa on the left bank of the Nile. As stated in his will, the Aga Khan was buried here two years after his death, in the mausoleum built above the white house where his widow, the Begum, still lives. The mausoleum was built in pink limestone, on the model of the Cairo mosque of El-Guyushi, in the unadorned Fatimid style. Inside, the tomb is in white Carrara marble, with inscriptions from the Koran on the sides, so beautifully engraved they look like embroidery. A fresh red rose has been laid on his tomb every day since his burial.

The most usual and characteristic way of reaching the monastery of St. Simeon continues to be the camel.

Panorama of Deir Amba Samaan, the fortified monastery of St. Simeon.

MONASTERY OF ST. SIMEON

There were once cultivated fields as far as the Nile in this small valley. Today the imposing ruins of this monastery, a real true fortress, are set against the savage beauty of the desert.

The Deir Amba Samaan (as it is called in Arab) is one of the largest and best preserved Coptic monasteries in all of Egypt. It was built between the 6th and 8th centuries and the death of the bishop Hadra. It could house up to 300 monks and offer shelter to hundreds and hundreds of pilgrims. After a life of almost five hundred years, the Arabs destroyed it in 1321, killing many of the monks and driving out the survivors. The surrounding wall of stone and unbaked brick flanked by towers two meters high lend it a majestic solemn air which induces respect and awe.

Inside, the convent was conceived of as a real city in miniature. On the first level is the tripartite church with an apse with three chapels. Traces of frescoes depciting the Pantokrator and twenty-four seated saints are still visible. Above each saint is painted a letter of the Coptic alphabet. A staircase leads to the second floor, where the real monastery is, with a long corridor on which the monks' cells

The church chapel with its three niches: a fresco of Christ Pantokrator is in the central niche.

The long corridor onto which the cells of the monks face and a view of the powerful encircling wall.

face and the service rooms for the community, such as kitchen, bakery, cellar, etc.

If we cimb to the top of the walls, the desert stretches out in all its majesty. All around is sand, crossed slowly by the camels which bring the tourists here. At the back of the valley we are struck by the shocking contrast of Aswan overlooking the blue waters of the Nile and the white feluccas lazily waiting, half hidden in the green of the palm groves. It is particularly lovely to approach the monastery at sunset, when the ruins take on a rosy hue that blends in with the sand from which they seem to emerge as if by magic.

The necropolis of Aswan, on the left bank of the
Nile, in a haunting nocturnal vision.

The « top of the winds » (Qubbet el Hawa) in
which the forty hypogeum tombs of the princes
of Elephantine are excavated.

NECROPOLIS OF THE PRINCES

The left bank of the Nile is dominated by the hill
called Qubett el Hawa (the « top of the winds »)
with a small ruined temple at its summit, offering
an unforgettable spectacle: Aswan, the mass of
rocks which form the First Cataract and the desert
all around. Right underfoot are the around forty
tombs that go to make up the interesting necropolis
of the princes of Elephantine.

Contemporaries of the last pharaohs of the Old
Kingdom, these dignitaries had their tombs dug into
the rock. Entrance was via a steep ramp which
served to haul up the sarcophagus. The layout of
the tomb is generally very schematic: a rectangular
chamber with pillars, the chapel and the sarcophagus room. The decoration is also extremely simple
and consists only of paintings, for the limestone in
which the tomb was cut was not suitable for low
reliefs.

The stairs leading to the tombs.

The sarcophagus of the dead prince was hoisted up on this ramp overhanging the Nile.

Exterior of the tomb of Heqa-ib, preceded by a large court and two tall conical pillars.

Painting inside the tomb of Heqa-ib with scenes of hunting and fishing.

Tomb of Heqa- ib — Discovered in 1947, this tomb belonged to Heqa-ib, a dignitary about whom we know only that he was governor of Elephantine at the end of the Old Kingdom, during the 6th dynasty. Whatever popularity he may have had was posthumous for he was deified for some unknown reason and the small temple already seen on the Elephantine Island near the temple of Khnum was erected in his honor. His tomb is not large nor does it have any outstanding decoration. When it was discovered, however, about sixty steles dedicated to him were found in the court.

Tombs of Mekhu and Sabni — These two tombs at the southernmost end of the necropolis are inter-communicating for their owners were father and son. Mekhu, « hereditary prince » and « only friend » during the 6th dynasty, had gone south as far as the Second Cataract and during the journey encountered death. His son Sabni, as can be read on the sides of the entrance to the second tomb, organized an expedition to go in search of his father's body and bring it back home where solemn funeral rites were celebrated, with expert embalmers called in to mummify him.

Mekhu's tomb has a vast hall with three rows of six columns each. At the center between two pillars is a block of granite which served as an offering table: to be noted are the symbols for bread and the drainage canals for the ritual libations. Sabni's tomb is divided by twelve pillars arranged in two rows and is decorated with scenes of hunting and fishing.

More scenes of hunting and fishing frescoes in the tomb of Heqa-ib.

The exterior of the tomb of Mekhu and Sabni.

Frescoes inside the tomb with scenes of offering and hunting.

The exterior of the tomb of Sirenpowet I and part of a boat decorated with hieroglyphs.

Two pictures of the decoration inside the tomb.

Tomb of Sirenpowet I — Very little remains of this tomb in which the son of Satseni, a 12th- dynasty prince at the time of Amenemhet II, was buried to testify to the fact that it was the largest and most richly developed tomb in the entire necropolis. Even so, part of the enclosure and the entrance portal in limestone still exist, with fine bas-reliefs depicting the deceased prince, the « Superior of the prophets of Satis ». A portico with six piers was on the facade of the tomb. The interior consisted of a chamber with four pilasters which must originally have been richly decorated with paintings which are now in very poor condition: the scenes referred to daily life on land and sea.

The exterior and the interior of the tomb of Sirenpowet II: in the chapel at the back the son is shown paying homage to his father before a prepared table; on either side the prince and his wife.

Tomb of Sirenpowet II — The tomb, one of the best preserved, belonged to the « Superior of the prophets of Khnum » during the 12th dynasty. It consisted of a first chamber with six pillars, a gallery flanked by six niches each of which contained the mummylike statue of the deceased prince and a second square chamber with four pillars, each of which was decorated with a lovely image of Sirenpowet. After that comes the back chapel which is painted: the prince is shown with his small son rendering him homage before a table set with bread, sweets, fruit, even a duck and bunches of grapes. The adjacent wall is decorated with the figure of the wife of the prince, a priestess of Hathor, also shown seated before a prepared table.

The imposing unfinished obelisk and a detail showing the holes left by the quoins used in extracting the granite from the quarry.

UNFINISHED OBELISK

If this obelisk had been finished it would have been a candidate for the Guinness Book of Records. It would in fact have been over 41 meters high with a base of four meters and consequently a weight of 1,267 tons! But a crack in the granite, perhaps the result of a tremor, or the poor quality of the stone, brought the work to a halt and the obelisk remained as we see it now, abandoned on the ground near those granite quarries which tell us so much about how the ancient Egyptians cut the stone. Once the ancient quarries of Aswan stretched for more than six kilometers from the Nile. This was the stone the Egyptians favored in facing their pyramids, and since it was near the river, the stone could easily be loaded on the boats and carried upstream.

The incisions cut regularly into the rock provide indications of how the blocks of stone were quarried. Wooden wedges or quoins were inserted into these grooves, which marked the surface that was to be extracted. When the wedges were wet, the wood expanded and the quoins burst, splitting off the rock in the desired direction, with surfaces that were relatively smooth and ready for polishing.

HIGH DAM

About five kilometers south of the city the course of the Nile is barred by the Old Dam of Aswan (Es Saad, the dam), built by the English between 1898 and 1902 with an initial height of 30.5 meters and a capacity of a billion cubic meters of water. Before long this proved insufficient and in two stages (from 1907 to 1912 and from 1929 to 1934) the dam was enlarged to its present size: 41.5 meters high and with a capacity of five billion cubic meters of water. Still this was not enough to meet the demands of the Egyptian territory. The drama of Egypt is to be found in two numbers: 900,000 square kilometers of land of which only 38,000, not much more than 4%, can be cultivated. A new dam would not only increase the amount of farmland, but irrigation would become a reality and the annual production of electricity would be increased. It was thus decid-

The modern monument set up at some distance before the High Dam in memory of the enormous commitment of all those who worked on this truly pharaonic undertaking: the shape recalls a stylized lotus blossom.

Am image of the Saad el Aali, the High Dam: 3,600 meters long and 40 meters high, it has various observation points that permit an ample panorama over the gigantic hydro-electric turbines below and Lake Nasser.

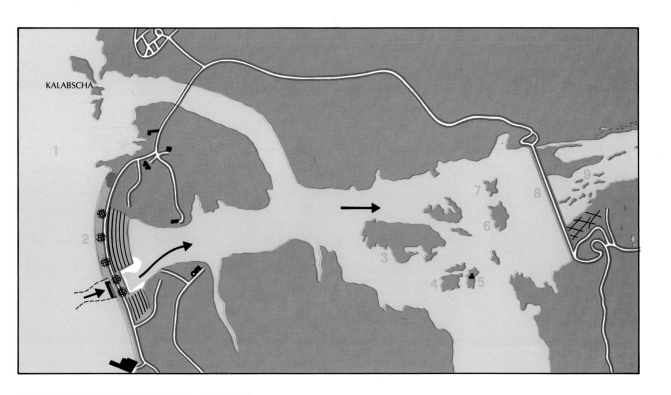

THE DAM COMPLEX AT ASWAN

1 - NASSER LAKE
2 - HIGH DAM (SAAD EL-AALI)
3 - ISLAND OF EL-HESA
4 - ISLAND OF BIGEH
5 - ISLAND OF PHILAE

6 - ISLAND OF AGILKIA
7 - ISLAND OF KONOSSO
8 - OLD DAM (ES-SAAD)
9 - FIRST CATARACT

MINIMUM HEIGHT
ABOVE SEA LEVEL

NORMAL HEIGHT
ABOVE SEA LEVEL

CROSS SECTION OF THE HIGH DAM

ROCK MUCK

DUNE SAND

ROCK MUCK SLUICED WITH SAND

VIBRATED DUNE SAND

ANTI FILTER CURTAIN

ed to embark upon the construction of a new barrier in the river, called the « barrier against hunger », a new dam which as Nasser said « would set Egypt on the road to modernity ».

The High Dam (Saad el Aali) is about eight kilometers upstream from the Old. The Soviet Union was entrusted with the study of the project. Construction began in January 1960; on May 14, 1964 the waters of the Nile were deviated into a branch canal and in 1972 the work — of pharaonic dimensions — could be considered finished. The body of water thus formed, Lake Nasser, is 500 kilometers long (150 of which are in Sudanese territory) and has a capacity of 157 billion cubic meters of water: second only to the dam of Kariba on the Zambesi River.

The creation of this artificial basin obviously resulted in radical modifications in the landscape and in the environment. First of all the numerous Nubian villages in the area involved had to be evacuated. Then attention was centered on the dramatic situation of the many important archaeological sites in Nubia which would inevitably have been submerged. When it was realized that the economic improvement of Egypt meant the irreparable destruction of its archaeological inheritance, UNESCO reacted to the call for aid launched by the Egyptian and Sudanese governments and set in motion a gigantic campaign to raise the funds needed to save the threatened temples.

Not one of the fourteen temples involved has been preserved on its original site: once dismantled, they have been faithfully reconstructed elsewhere.

Among these, the temple of Kalabsha, clearly visible from the High Dam, is one of the finest and best preserved.

A view of Lake Nasser from the Aswan Dam presents us on the right with one of the loveliest Nubian temples, Kalabsha. Threatened by the waters of the lake when the great dam was constructed, it was removed from its original site and rebuilt here by a German archaeological mission. Unfortunately the only way to reach it at present is with a tiny rowboat - a pity, for its beauty and grandeur merit so much more.

The pylon of the temple of Kalabsha, or Mandulis.

KALABSHA

Kalabsha was the ancient Talmis, the most important city of the Dodecascheno (« Land of the twelve miles »), about forty kilometers south from where it is now. The god Mandulis was worshipped there — a god wearing a complicated diadem on his head — and whom the Egyptians identified with Horus. In importance and size, the sanctuary dedicated to this local god was second only to Abu Simbel. Seventy-one meters long and thirty-five wide, it was defined by the English writer Amelia Edwards as the « Karnak of Nubia ». Of the so-called « inner sanctuary type » the temple was built on an earlier one from the times of Amenophis II. The plan includes a pylon, a court, a pronaos and a naos formed of three successive chambers. The pylon is 41 meters high and one can climb to the top to admire the beautiful panorama of the High Dam and Lake Nasser. The pylon leads to the paved court where the worshippers could go on the great festivals. It is surrounded on three sides by a porch and columns which fell when an earthquake struck but which were partially reconstructed when the temple was recomposed. Then comes the pronaos which had twelve columns with bell capitals. The facade is decorated with various inscriptions. One, in Greek, narrates how Silco, king of Ethiopia in the middle of the 6th century A.D., had come to destroy Talmis, inhabited by his enemies. Another inscription, also in Greek, notes the decree emanated by the governor Aurelio Besarione who around the

The facade of the hypostyle hall, seen from the front and above, with its bell capitals and screen walls. The decoration was unfortunately never finished.

Two decorations of the temple, with representations of Horus and Mandulis.

year 250 ordered, on religious grounds, all the swineherds and their pigs to leave the temple within fifteen days. The interior of the pronaos is also decorated with the figures of Mandulis, Thot, Horus, etc. Up to the end of the 19th century the decorations still had their original colors. Nowadays, unfortunately, all trace has been lost and we must trust in the descriptions and drawings of ancient travelers who were lucky enough to see them and to copy them. After the pronaos come the three chambers which formed the naos, each one lower than the one before, and with columns supporting the ceiling. In the cell which contained the statue of Mandulis interesting decorations, characterized by a certain freshness of execution, are still extant.

Only the first of the encircling walls the temple originally had is still extant. A sort of spacious sentry corridor, which also contains a nilometer, is set between the stone wall and that of the temple. To the west, on the external wall, is an enormous relief of Mandulis: he is shown twice, on the right in his real aspect and on the left in his divine aspect.

At the time of the great rescue of the Nubian temples, Kalabsha was « turned over » to the technicians of the German Federal Republic who dismantled it into 13,000 blocks and rebuilt it on this promontory, a stone sentinel for the endless expanse of Lake Nasser.

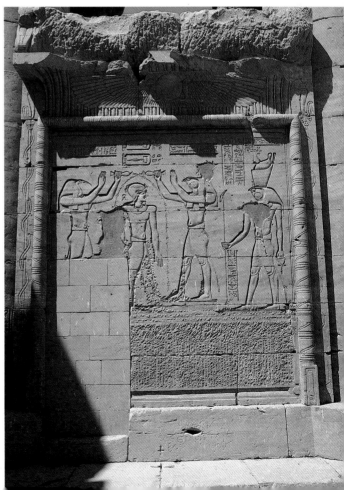

The small temple of Kertassi seen from above and a detail of the Hathor pillars.

KERTASSI

Erected on high ground above the Nile, the small temple of Kertassi was dedicated to Isis and originally was in the town of Tzitzis. It closely recalls Trajan's Kiosk at Philae, of rectangular form, with columns and composite capitals joined by screen walls and with two large Hathor pillars at the portal. Only one of the architraves which once supported the roof — no longer there — is still exant and it has numerous inscriptions.

BEIT EL WALI

The rock-cut temple of Beit el Wali is not far from the large temple of Kalabsha. The name means « House of the Governor » and it was built by the viceroy of Kush (Upper Nubia) for Ramses II. It is a speos cut into the mountain and consists of only two chambers, a long hall and the sanctuary, both preceded by an open court, the walls of which are decorated in relief with military scenes that commemorate the victorious campaigns of Ramses II: Syrian and Libyan on the right wall and Ethiopian on the left wall. The vestibule, which was transformed into a church in the 6th century, has two proto-Dorian columns holding up the ceiling: here the reliefs of religious scenes still have their original colors fairly well preserved. Ramses II is shown before the hawk-headed Horus and Selkis, and the pharaoh is also seen making offerings to the holy triad of Khnum, Satis and Anukis.

One of the frescoes inside depicting the pharaoh in the act of killing an enemy.

The entrance to the small rock-cut temple of Beit el Wali: the scene on the right wall depicts the victory of Ramses II over the Syrians and Libyans.

The brightly colored houses of the Nubian village on the island of Siheyl.

Some of the around 200 rock inscriptions on the island of Siheyl: the most important is number 81, known as the « stele of famine ».

ISLAND OF SIHEYL

Upstream, a few kilometers from Aswan, is the First Cataract of the Nile, a vast zone of turbulant waters and whirlpools with innumerable rocks and islets. Seen from above, the cataract really looks like primordial chaos. River traffic was interrupted here: the boats unloaded their camels which went round the rocks carrying the goods, and went on greatly lightened, passing with agility through the narrow passages formed by the islets. The pharaoh Sesostris III, in the 12th dynasty, had had a canal dug parallel to the river to allow the ships to continue their journey towards the farthest parts of Nubia.

Travelers, soldiers, traders: all left here traces of their passage in the dozens and dozens of graffiti which cover the black granite on Siheyl. The island was sacred to Anukis, represented in female form and with plumes on her head, and to whom a temple that is no longer extant was dedicated. All that is left are the remains of two other small temples, one from the times of Amenophis II (18th dynasty) and the other from the times of Ptolemy XIV Philopator. There are about two hundred inscriptions on the island, and they range from the 6th dynasty to the Ptolemaic period. The most interesting is no. 81, known also as the « stele of famine » of the Ptolemaic period. It refers to the terrible famine which had been flailing Egypt for seven years and how the pharaoh Zoser thanked Khnum with the erection of a temple because the god had finally sent a flood. The text of this stele made it possible to identify Zoser as the pharaoh who had the step pyramid in Saqqara built.

After the visit to the graffiti, it will be a pleasure to stop even briefly in a Nubian house: inside it is cool and a cup of mint tea is just the thing to reward the fatigues of this outing!

View from on high of the islet of Agilkia, on which the complex of temples formerly on Philae has been recomposed.

The left flank of the large temple of Isis, with the first and second pylon and, below, Trajan's pavilion, on the opposite side of the island.

PHILAE

History

In the midst of a fascinating landscape of granite rocks, the sacred island, domain of the goddess Isis, raises its columns and pillars towards the cloudless sky, giving one the impression of being in a purely imaginary place. The temple of Philae is one of the three best preserved Ptolemaic temples, the other two are those of Edfu and Dendera.

Philae was the largest of the three islands at the south end of the group of rocks that comprise the First Cataract, and is 400 meters long and 135 meters wide. The name itself reveals its unique geographic position: Pilak in fact, as it was called in the ancient texts, meant « the corner island » or « the end island ». For originally Philae was on the east bank of the Nile, in the corner of a small bay, and also at the southermost tip of the First Cataract. Of the other two islets, Bigeh (today partially sub-

merged) was particularly sacred for it was the place of eternal sleep for Osiris and therefore out of bounds to all human beings. Only those priests who came by boat from Philae were allowed there where they celebrated their sacred rites on the 360 offering tables which indicated where Osiris was buried. The temples on Philae were dedicated to his bride Isis who with the force of her love had recomposed his scattered limbs and resuscitated him. The cult of the goddess on this island dates to extremely ancient times and it was a tradition that at least once a year the Egyptians go in pilgrimage to the sacred island. It was not until A.D. 535, under the reign of Justinian, that the priests dedicated to the cult were removed.

The third islet is Agilkia: and this is where we can now admire the temple complex which was originally on Philae, barely 500 meters away.

The sacred island, in fact, was above water through-

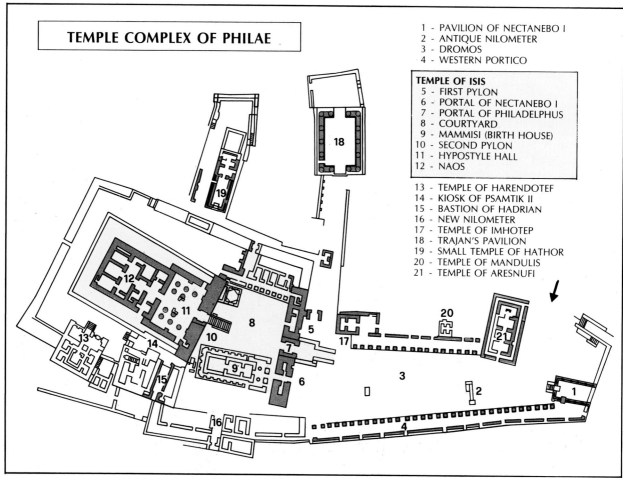

TEMPLE COMPLEX OF PHILAE

1 - PAVILION OF NECTANEBO I
2 - ANTIQUE NILOMETER
3 - DROMOS
4 - WESTERN PORTICO

TEMPLE OF ISIS
5 - FIRST PYLON
6 - PORTAL OF NECTANEBO I
7 - PORTAL OF PHILADELPHUS
8 - COURTYARD
9 - MAMMISI (BIRTH HOUSE)
10 - SECOND PYLON
11 - HYPOSTYLE HALL
12 - NAOS

13 - TEMPLE OF HARENDOTEF
14 - KIOSK OF PSAMTIK II
15 - BASTION OF HADRIAN
16 - NEW NILOMETER
17 - TEMPLE OF IMHOTEP
18 - TRAJAN'S PAVILION
19 - SMALL TEMPLE OF HATHOR
20 - TEMPLE OF MANDULIS
21 - TEMPLE OF ARESNUFI

Two views of the pavilion of Nectanebo I, with the bell columns and Hathor capitals.

out the year until 1898. With the construction of the Old Dam, it remained submerged by the artificial lake most of the year. Only in August and September when the lock-gates of the dam were opened to alleviate the pressure of the flood waters, did the island emerge from the waters so it could be visited. The construction of the High Dam put Philae in a critical situation: the sacred island would have found itself in a closed basin in which the waters, no longer twenty meters high as before but only four, would have created a continual ebb and flow that with the passing of the years would have inevitably eroded the foundations of the temples which sooner or later would have fallen.

They were, therefore, between 1972 and 1980, dismantled and rebuilt on this islet (where the topography of Philae was recreated) in a position that was higher up with respect to the waters of the lake.

The temple complex includes the pavilion of Nectanebo, the monumental temple of Isis with its annexes, the charming pavilion of Trajan and the small Hathor temple.

The spacious dromos cut off at the back by the first pylon of the temple of Isis and as David Roberts painted it. The view of Philae on the left is also due to the same artist.

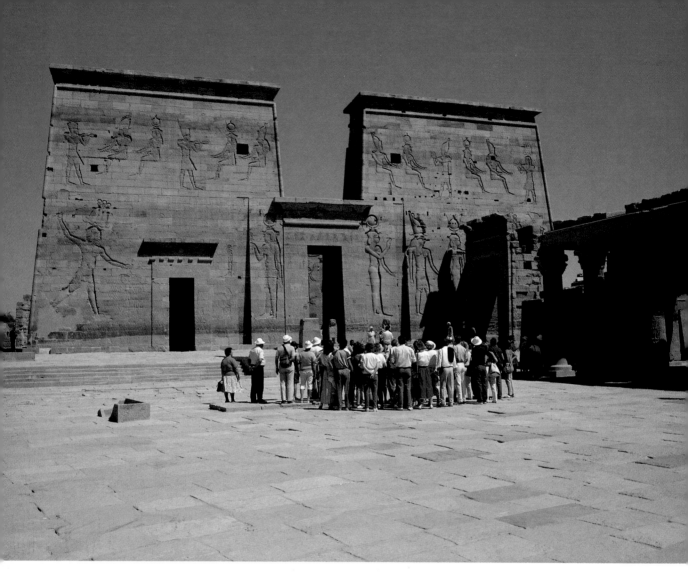

A general view of the first pylon of the temple of Isis.

A detail of the first pylon, with the gigantic figures of Isis and Horus.

Visit

The landing-stage for the boats that bring the tourists to visit the complex of Philae lies at the southwest tip of the island.

The first building to be encountered is the **pavilion of Nectanebo I**, a rectangular portico with fourteen bell columns and Hathor capitals: here the broad face of the goddess also has the ears of a cow (fairly common in all late capitals) so that it contemporaneously has the form of a sistrum, the favorite musical instrument of Isis, and is also a symbol of Ihi, Hathor's young son. Since the pavilion dates to the 4th century B.C. it can be considered the oldest temple in the complex. In front is the large **dromos**, with porticoes on either side. The right hand one was never finished; that on the left has 32 columns

with traces of decoration on the ceiling and offering scenes on the colums and the back wall. The plant-shaped capitals differ one from the other.

The perspective is now scenographically brought to a close by the **temple of Isis**, with its monumental *first pylon*: it is 18 meters high and 45.5 meters wide and consists of two massive towers which flank the portal. On the tower the pharaoh Ptolomy XI Neos Dionysos grasps, in the customary pose, the prisoners by the hair and prepares to sacrifice them to the gods Isis, Horus and Hathor. In the left tower the reliefs which show the pharaoh armed with a staff and about to kill the enemy prisoners are in poorer condition. Passing between the two pylons, under the portal built by Nectanebo I whose cartouches can be seen, we find on the right a relief commemorating the French victory over the Mame-

lukes in the « an VII de la République » (1799). We are now in the temple court with the back wall formed by the second pylon, the right by a porticoed building with various annexes used by the priests. The elegant *Mammisi temple* on the left side is a peripteral building (surrounded on four sides by colums with capitals terminating in Hathor sistrums), with three rooms preceded by a naos. Isis and her son Horus, whose birth, childhood and education are narrated in the fine decorations, were worshipped in the Mammisi. Also to be noted above on the outer facade, the reproduction of the text of the Rosetta stone which made it possible to decipher Egyptian hieroglyphics. The *second pylon* is higher (22 meters high and 32 wide) than but not exactly

Another detail of pylon with Pharaoh offering to gods Isis and Horus.

The pharaoh shown grasping the prisoners by the hair as he prepares to kill them.

General view and detail of the so-called gate of Ptolemy, set against the first pylon.

The first court of the temple of Isis: the internal colonnade and a view of the second pylon.

The second pylon, with the customary images of the pharaoh before Isis and Horus.

The block of granite set against the righthand tower of the second pylon.

parallel to the first. On the facade it also has the customary scene of Pharaoh Ptolemy XI Neos Dionysos massacring the prisoners before the gods. On the right an enormous block of granite commemorates a donation of lands that Ptolemy VI made to the temple. A few steps lead to the *hypostyle hall*, ten colums with polychrome floral capitals and traces of decoration on the ceiling: symbols of Upper and Lower Egypt, sun boats, astronomical symbols. In the 6th century at the time of the bishop Theodorus, the pronaos was transformed into a Christian church as witnessed by the many Coptic crosses engraved on the walls. From here access is gained to the naos, which consists of twelve rooms and a crypt, all decorated with liturgic scenes. After this came the sanctuary, containing the boat with the image of the goddess. A staircase leads to the terrace where a vestibule and a chamber comprise the funerary chapel of Osiris: the decoration narrates the Osiris cycle with the death, funeral and magical rites and the resurrection of the god. While most of the decorations at Philae regard sacred rites and tributes to the gods, there is one that stands out for its originality and the atypicality of the subject represented. This is the so-called gate or **bastion of Hadrian**, an aedicule that dates to Antonine times and that is situated in the western wing of the temple of Isis, on a level with the second pylon. Inside the gate, on the north wall, a relief demonstrates the Egyptian concept of the source of the Nile. In fact Hapis, the deification of the Upper and Lower Nile, is shown in an anthropomorphic and hermaphroditic form. The god is show in a cave surrounded by a serpent and he holds two vases from which water flows. In fact, the ancient Egyptians believed that the source of the Nile was in the

neighborhood of the First Cataract near a mountain called Mu Hapi (meaning « water of Hapi »). The annual rites in honor of the god were celebrated by the pharaoh himself and began in the middle of June when the star Sotis marked the beginning of the river flood.

On the other side, that is on the right side of the temple of Isis, is another jewel of this great Ptolemaic complex of Philae: **Trajan's pavilion**. Overlooking the river, extremely elegant and finely proportioned, it has in a sense become the symbol of the entire island. In olden times this was where the sacred barge with the statue of Isis landed during the magnificent processions on the river. Rebuilt by the emperor Trajan, the rectangular kiosk has fourteen columns with bell capitals and screen walls, two of which are decorated with scenes representing Trajan making offerings to Isis, Osiris

A corner of the hypostyle hall, the so-called gate or bastion of Hadrian and a detail of the reliefs inside.

The inside of the court as painted by David Roberts.

The right side of the temple of Isis with the passage of Tiberius and a detail of the gate.

A detail of the decoration of the small temple of Hathor, depicting a monkey playing a musical instrument.

The elegant pavilion of Trajan, with its fourteen bell columns.

and Horus.

Beyond the kiosk is the **small temple to Hathor**, erected by Ptolemy VI Philometer and Evergete II, but decorated later by Augustus. Some of the reliefs are rather amusing and show, among other things, a priest playing the double flute and some monkeys dancing while one plays the lute.

Philae represents a perfect synthesis of the Egyptian, Greek and Roman civilizations: here architecture and design are one. It suffices to remember that once, before the waters of the Old Dam washed them clean, all the capitals were painted in brilliant colors — blue, red, yellow and green — as witnessed by the paintings of those travelers who saw them before the temple was submerged in the artificial basin of Aswan. Despite the fact that all the original color has disappeared, Philae remains that masterpiece of grace and enchantment, as Amelia Edwards wrote, a marvelous example of elegance and charm, which led Pierre Loti to call it the « pearl of Egypt ».

In the picture below, the architectural complex as seen and painted in 1839 by David Roberts.

Panorama of the entire complex of rock-cut temples of Abu Simbel. Note on the left the Great Temple of Ramses II and on the right that of Hathor.

ABU SIMBEL

History

In the heart of the Nubian territory, almost on the borders of Sudan and about 300 kilometers from Aswan, is the most beautiful and imposing construction of the greatest pharaoh in Egyptian history: Abu Simbel, the temple that in theory was dedicated to the triad Amon-Ra, Harmakes, and Ptah, but which was to all extents erected solely to glorify in the centuries its constructor, Ramses II the Great. Abu Simbel is not only one of the most beautiful temples in Egypt — it is without doubt the most unusual and majestic — but it is also the symbol of the gigantic rescue operation involving all the fourteen Nubian temples threatened by Lake Nasser. Ybsambul, as it was called, had been long forgotten and once more saw the light of day in the last century when on May 22, 1813, the Swiss Johann Ludwig Burckhardt by chance saw the upper parts of four stone giants emerge almost as if by magic from the sand. On August 1, 1817, the Italian, Giovanni Battista Belzoni, freed the upper part of a doorway from the sand and found the entrance. After him travelers, scholars, archaeologists, tourists, came by the hundreds to admire the architectural masterpiece of Ramses II, free at last. The danger that it might disappear under the waters of Lake Nasser became a case that echoed throughout the world. While Abu Simbel was the most beautiful and the most imposing of the temples of Nubia, it was also the most difficult to save on account of the material in which it was sculpted, the site and the structure in which it had been conceived. Despite all this, here too man's will coupled with the wonders of technology succeeded — as we shall see — in saving the temple with one of the most unbelievable works of dismantlement and reconstruction that archaeology had ever been involved in and in perpetuating its memory throughout the centuries.

71

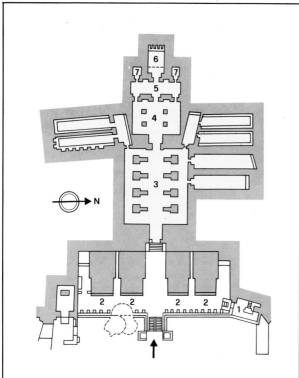

The four colossi of Ramses II and a detail of the two statues on the right: note the graffiti on the legs left by 19th-century tourists. From page 74 to page 77: four details of the statues of Ramses II.

GREAT TEMPLE OF ABU SIMBEL

1 - SANCTUARY OF THE SUN
2 - STATUE OF RAMSES II
3 - PRONAOS
4 - HYPOSTYLE HALL
5 - VESTIBULE
6 - SANCTUARY
7 - CHAPELS

A detail of the base of the facade.
Note the cartouches of the king at
the center.

When the colossi were still half
covered with sand, travelers of old
from various periods liked to leave
their signatures on the soft stone of
the facade.

Visit

The rock-cut temple of Abu Simbel is actually nothing but the transferral into rock of the architectural elements of the Egyptian so-called inner sanctuary temple.

The facade, carved into the mountain, is 38 meters long and 31 meters high and is framed by a convex molding of the « torus » type. It is surmounted by a cornice with uraei (representations of the sacred asp) above which is a row of twenty-two seated baboons, each two and a half meters high, in high relief. Under the torus molding is a cornice engraved with dedicatory hieroglyphs, and below this, in a niche at the center of the facade, the large high relief figure of Ra-Horakhte with a falcon head, flanked by two low-relief figures of Ramses II.

Four colossol **seated statues of Ramses II** replace the supporting columns of the facade. In their monumentality they perfectly reproduce the somatic features of the sovereign. Twenty meters high and more than four meters from ear to ear, with the line of the quietly smiling lips measuring over a meter, the pharaoh is shown with his hands resting on his thighs, the double crown on his head and the heavy nemes on either side of his face. The second statue is broken and part of the head and trunk are lying

The statue of Ra Horakhete with a falcon head and the row of 22 seated baboons and a detail of Ramses II.

A small dedicatory stele set in front of the entrance to the Great Temple.

The base of the terrace is decorated with reliefs depicting Negro and Asiatic prisoners of Ramses II.

One of the custodians of the Great Temple holds the large ankh-shaped key.

Asiatic prisoners on the base of the seats: above, the statue of Nofretari set against the leg of her husband Ramses.

on the ground.

Other statues are sculptured between the legs of each colossus. They represent members of the royal family, including the daughters (and his wives) Nebet Taui and Bent Anat, his mother Tuya, his wife Nofretari, his son Amen her Kopechef, his other daughter Merit Amen who was also married. On the base and sides of the chairs Negro and Asiatic prisoners are depicted.

A « multitude of workers brought into imprisonment by his sword » worked on this monumental facade, under the orders of the head of the sculptors, whose name was Pyay, as we read inside the temple. The work of the sculptors was followed by that of the painters: in the time of Ramses the temple must have been brightly colored.

From the blinding light of day we now pass into the interior where the half light creates a mysterious evocative atmosphere.

The **pronaos** is a vast rectangular hall, 18 meters long and 16.70 meters wide. There are eight Osiris pillars, each ten meters high, arranged in two rows and depicting Osiris with the features of Ramses. The colossi on the left wear the white crown of Upper Egypt, those on the right the « pschent » or double crown. Their arms are crossed over their breasts and hold the scepter and the flail. The ceiling of the nave is painted with the great vulture of the goddess Nekhbet, protectress of Upper Egypt, amd stars are painted over the side aisles.

The decoration of the walls celebrates the military glory of Ramses II. The most interesting and famous is the one on the north wall, where we can follow the various phases of the battle of Kadesh, including the pharaoh's military campaign against the Hittites in year V of his reign. The long epic poem, written by the court poet Pentaur, is engraved in hieroglyphics both here and on the walls of other tem-

General view of the pronaos, with the eight Osiris pillars and the sanctuary at the back.

The interior of the Great Temple painted by David Roberts.

A detail of the Osiris pillars.

Following pages: two frescoes showing the pharaoh with various gods, including the god Min who is shown as ithyphallic, his head adorned with two tall plumes and his arm raised and holding the flagellum.

General view of the sanctuary and detail of the four statues seated in the chapel: Harmakhis, the deified Ramses II, Amon Ra and Ptah.

ples, such as Luxor and Karnak.

The pronaos leads into a hypostyle hall, with four square pillars painted with images of the pharaoh before the various gods. The walls too are decorated with liturgic scenes, including the transportation of the sacred barge. Sixty-five meters from the entrance portal, in the heart of the mountain, is the **sanctuary**, the most intimate and secret place in the temple, a small room measuring four by seven meters. Here sits the statue of the deified Ramses II, together with the triad of Ptah, Amen Ra and Harmakhis. Regarding these statues, as early as the late 19th century it was realized that the entire temple was built according to a very precise scheme. Various scholars, first among whom François Champollion, had noted what was then called the « miracle

The facade of the Small Temple of Abu Simbel, or the temple of Hathor dedicated to Nofretari.

Detail of the entrance to the temple, flanked by the two large statues of Ramses.

of the sun ». Twice a year, at the solstices, the sun penetrates the entire length of the temple and floods the statues of Amon, Hamarkhis and the pharaoh with light. After about five minutes the light disappears and it is truly remarkable that Ptah is never struck by the rays of the sun, for Ptah is the god of darkness.

Eight other minor chambers open off the sides. This was where the Nubian tributes were stored.

Despite appearances, Abu Simbel is more than simply a matter of Rameses II glorifying himself. It suffices to leave the large temple and turn left: the **temple of Hathor** which the pharaoh had dedicated to Nofretari — his queen — not his only wife but certainly the best loved — strikes our eyes. Never in pharaonic Egypt had the consort of a sovereign been represented on the facade of a temple, as large as the statue of her husband right beside it. For her,

The simple interior of the temple of Hathor and a detail of one of the six Hathor pillars, with the head of the goddess above stories of the king and the queen.

for the Great Royal Consort, Nofretari-mery-en-Mut (« beloved of Mut ») Ramses had this temple cut in the « fine white and solid stone », small in size and of great harmony. The six statues, ten meters tall, with their left legs set slightly forward, seem to break out of the living rock as they move towards the light. Nofretari is shown as Hathor, with the horns of the sacred cow, the solar disk and two plumes. The divine consecration of the queen was also celebrated in the extremely simple **interior**, an almost square pronaos with six Hathor pillars set in two rows. The stories of Nofretari and Ramses

are engraved under the head of the goddess. The walls are also decorated with the customary scenes of offering and the massacre of the prisoners by the warrior king. Next comes the vestibule and, at the back, the customary sanctuary where the pharaoh honors Hathor, identified with his consort; the goddess, shown in the likeness of the sacred cow, set between two pillars, really seems to come out of the rock and is particularly striking.

How can one help but see a most human tender act of love on the part of the great pharaoh for his wife in this small temple.

The exterior of the two artificial hills against which the temples of Abu Simbel have been rebuilt, and part of the interior of the reinforced concrete dome of the Great Temple.

The rescuing of the Temples

For centuries the two rock-cut temples of Abu Simbel, lapped by the Nile, represented an architectural challenge to time. The same challenge was taken up two thousand years later by the engineers and technicians of the entire world when they attempted to save them. Many suggestions and projects for their preservation were made. In June 1963 the Swiss project was approved. It envisioned the complete removal of the mass of rock, cutting the temples into blocks and then recomposing them on higher ground. First of all 17,000 holes were bored in the rock and resin was injected to consolidate the stone. Thirty-three tons of resin and just as many iron clamps were needed. In the meanwhile the waters of the Nile rose faster than calculated and the job of cutting and transporting became a frenetic race against time. The monuments were sawn, some by hand, into 1036 blocks weighing on an average of thirty tons each, with an additional 1112 from the surrounding rock. The first block in the long series was raised on May 12, 1965, and marked as GA 1A01. Sixty-four meters higher up the two temples

Some arrive at Abu Simbel by sea plane and can thus land on the calm waters of Lake Nasser and admire the temples in all their imposing beauty from this vantage point.

Two unusual images for those who intend to reach Abu Simbel by car across the desert of Nubia: the straight ribbon of the road seems to move off into infinity. On either side of the asphalt, nothing but the yellow sands of the desert where the sun, when it is at its zenith, creates unforgettable mirages. Bus drivers like to stop and watch this spectacle to which they are so accustomed, but it is not quite the same for the tourists who are not used to these spaces and these dimensions which approach the absolute.

were being rebuilt exactly as they had originally been. But it was not simply a matter of setting them in a different site, for the weight of the artificial rock built above them would have crumbled them. Two enormous domes in reinforced concrete were planned to support the pressure of the mountain and protect the temples, like an enormous bell. The two domes would then have been covered with filling material, while sand and dust would gradually have closed the joints. On September 22, 1968, the great rock-cut ensemble was inaugurated for the second time in its history, while the waters of the Nile freely and slowly flowed into the caverns where the temples had been. And right on the dot, in February of 1969, the « miracle of the sun » was repeated when the sunbeams once more illuminated the gods seated inside the sanctuary. Ramses II had also won this last battle against the centuries and his architectural masterpiece and testament, despite everything, continued to exist.

CONTENTS

ISBN 88-7009-241-0